THE FAT KID COLORING BOOK

Created by Matthew Diomataris

COLOR TESTING PAGE

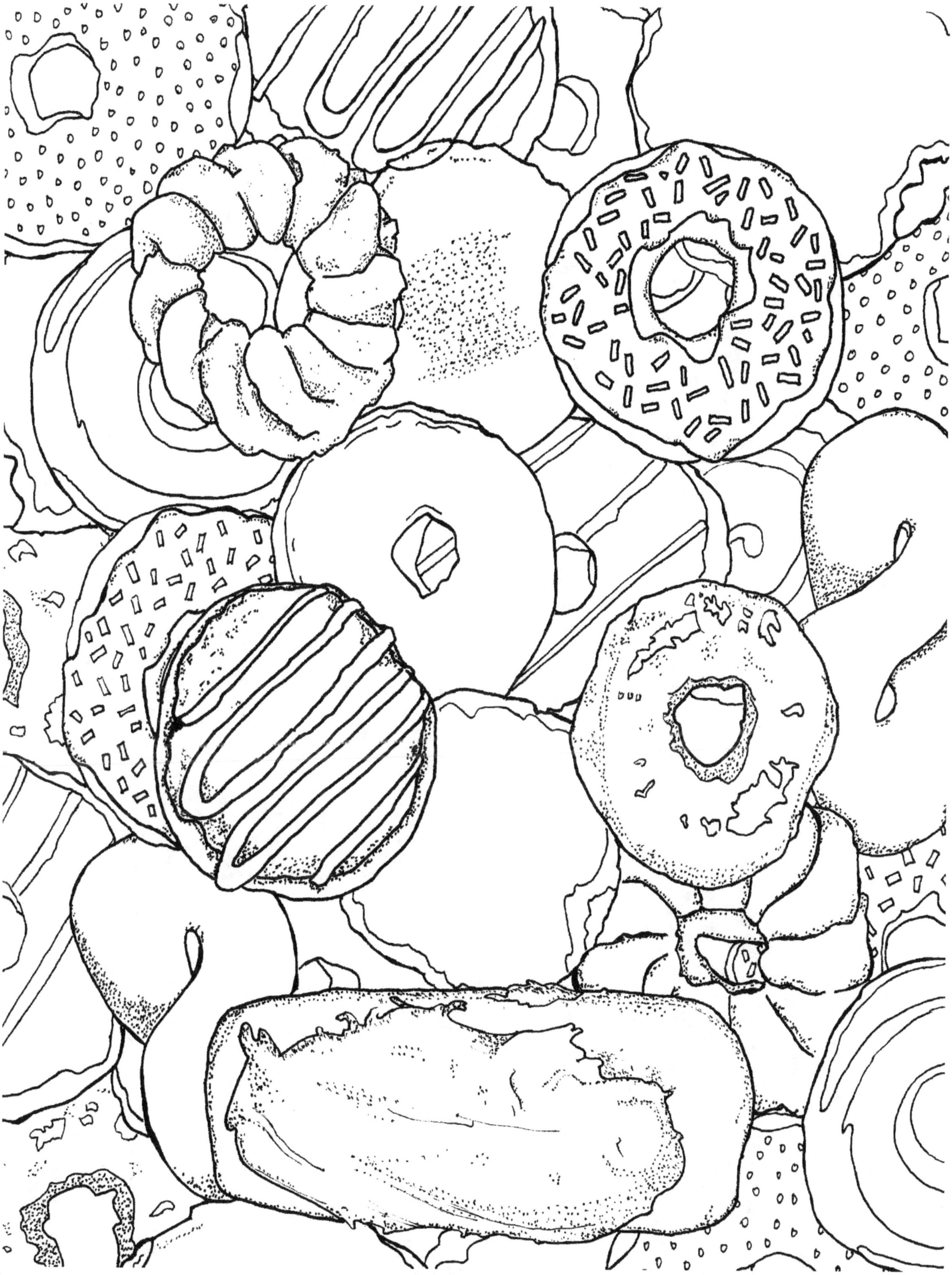

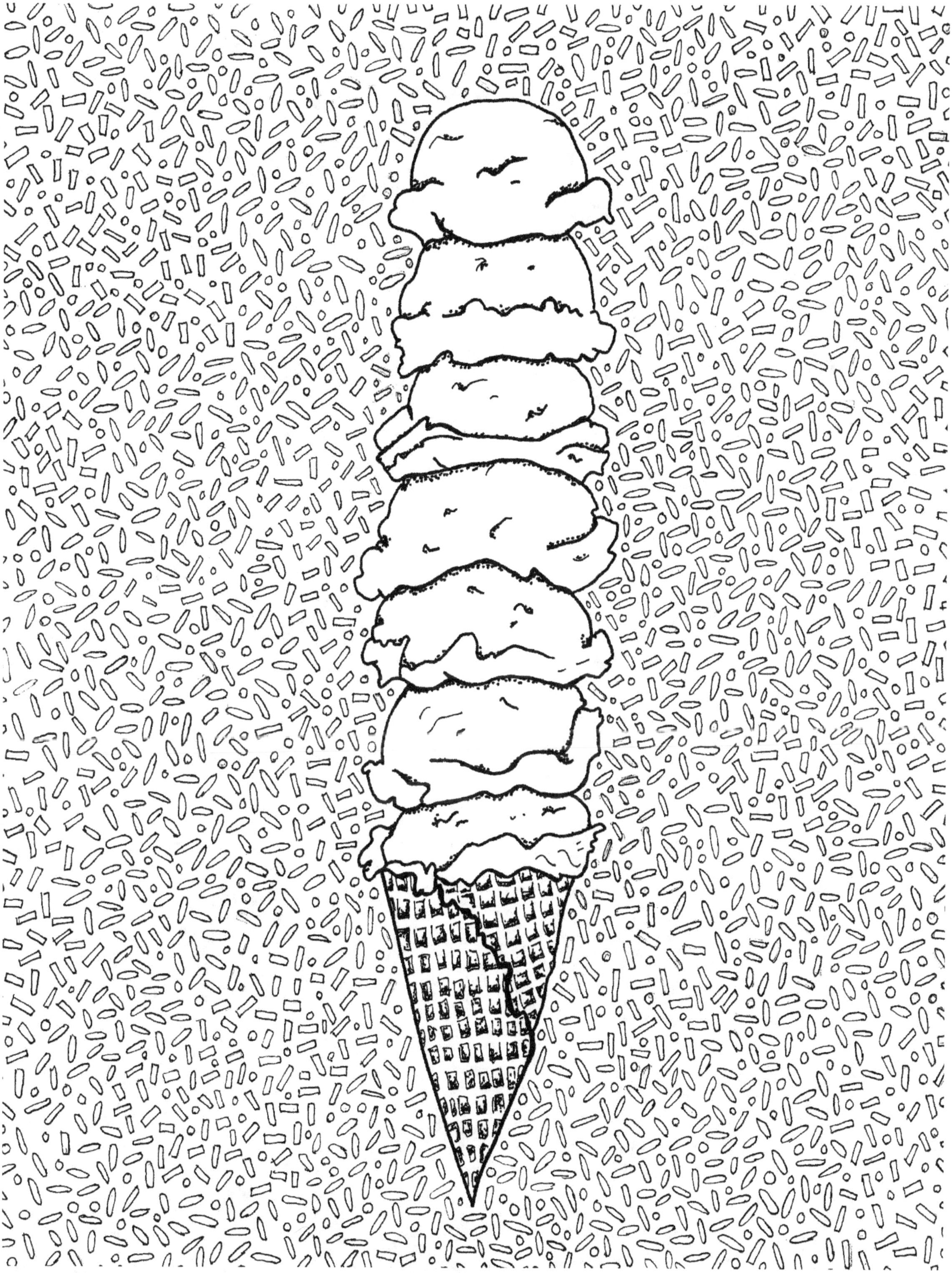

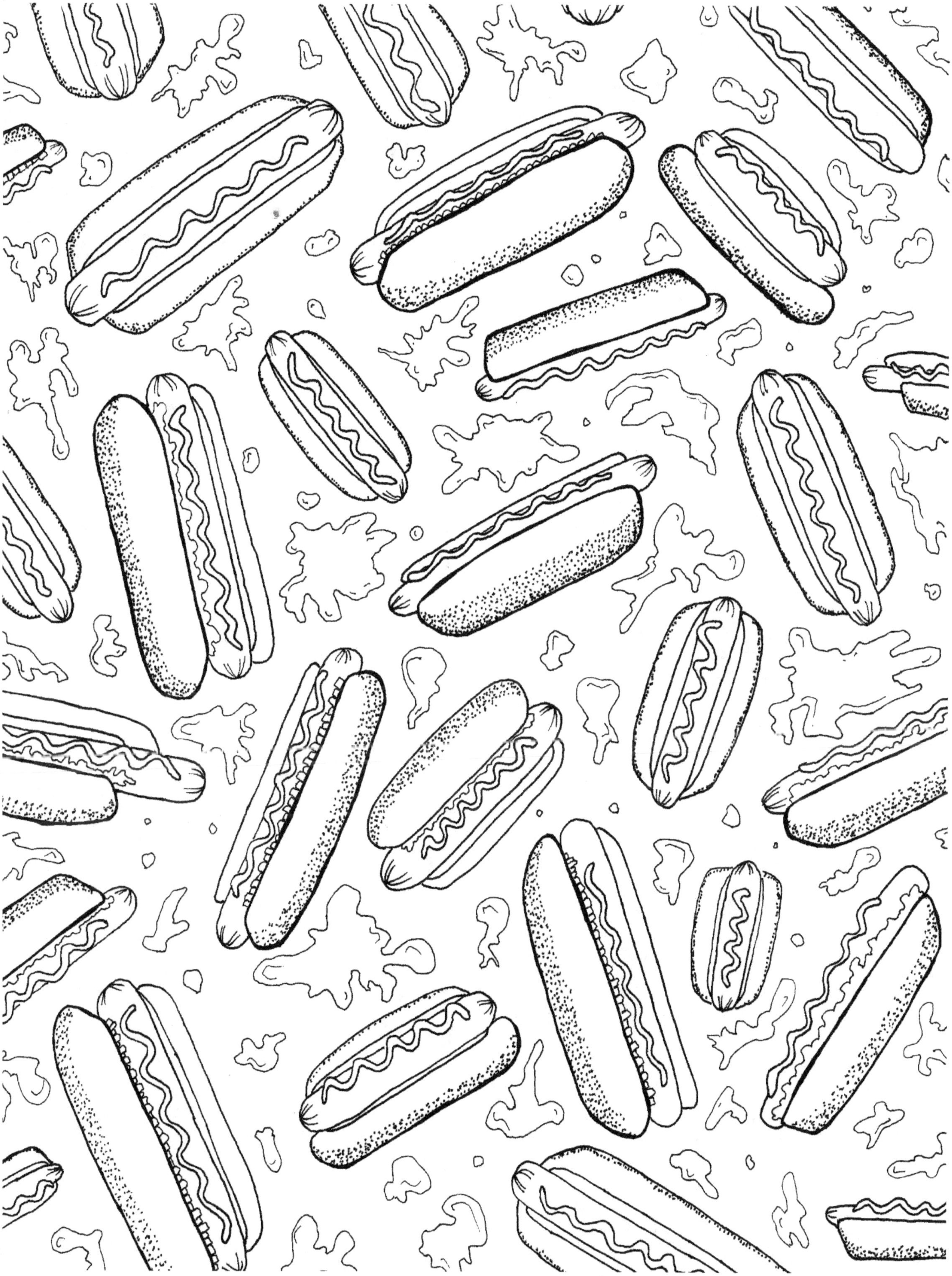

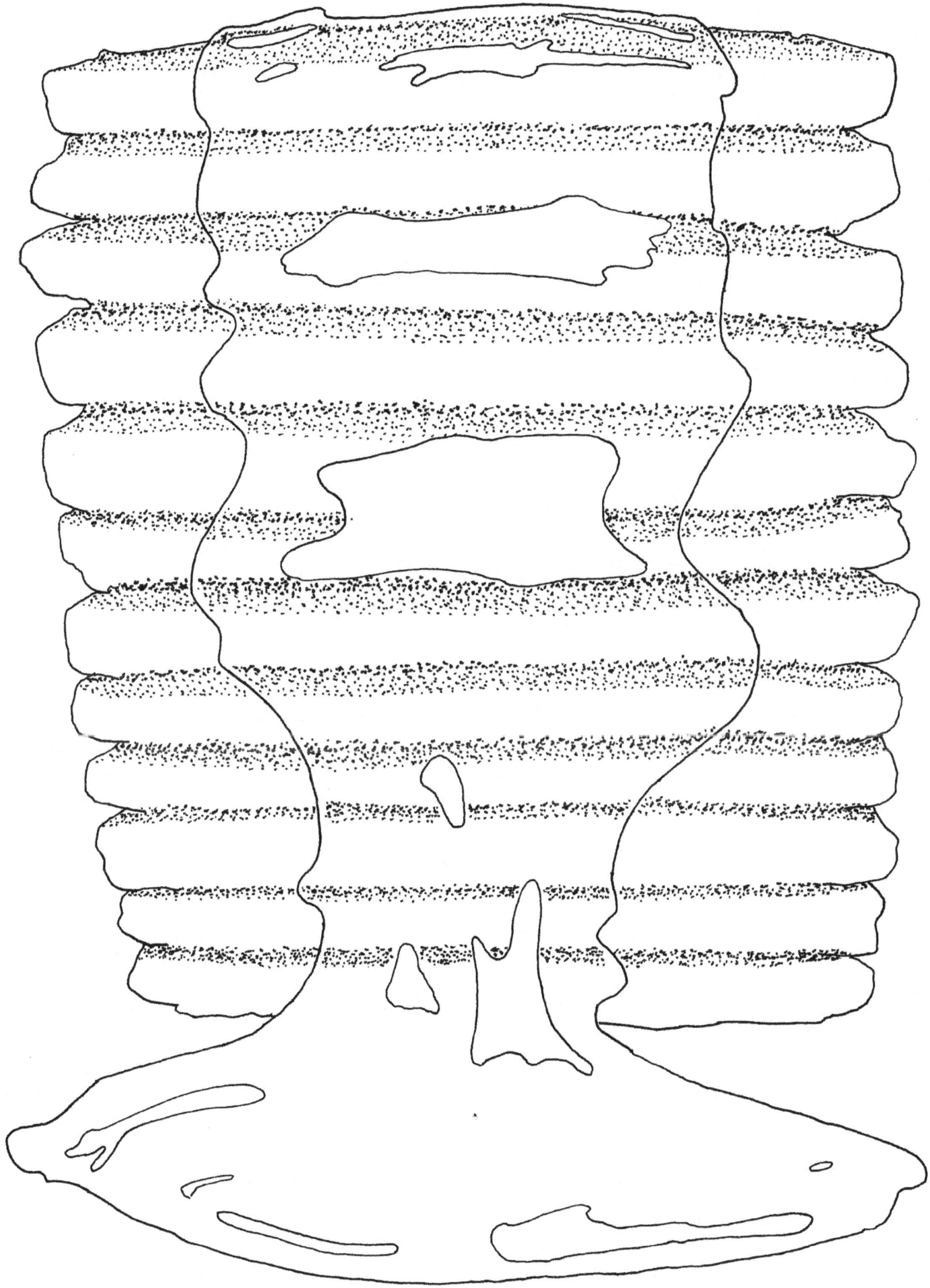

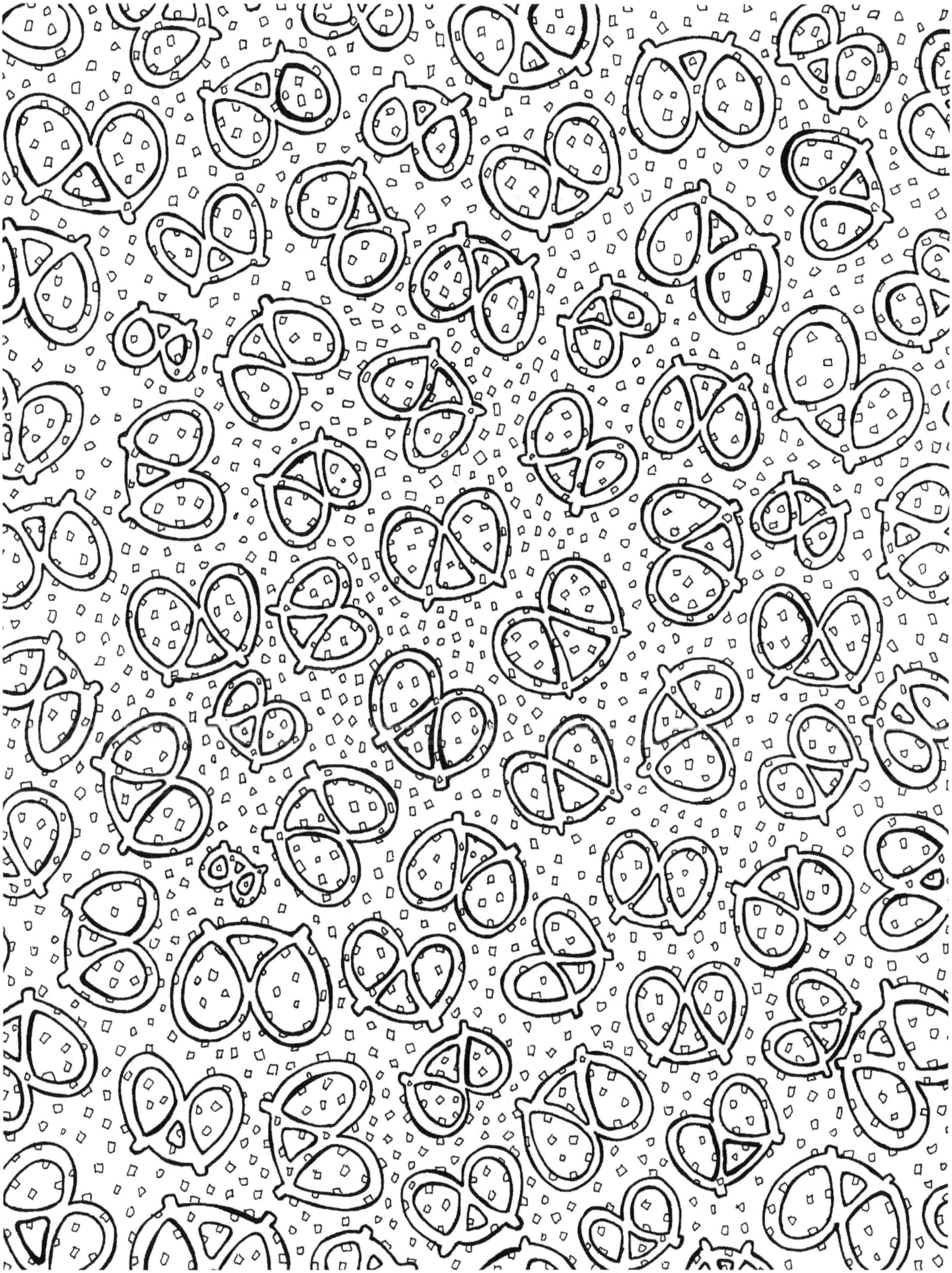

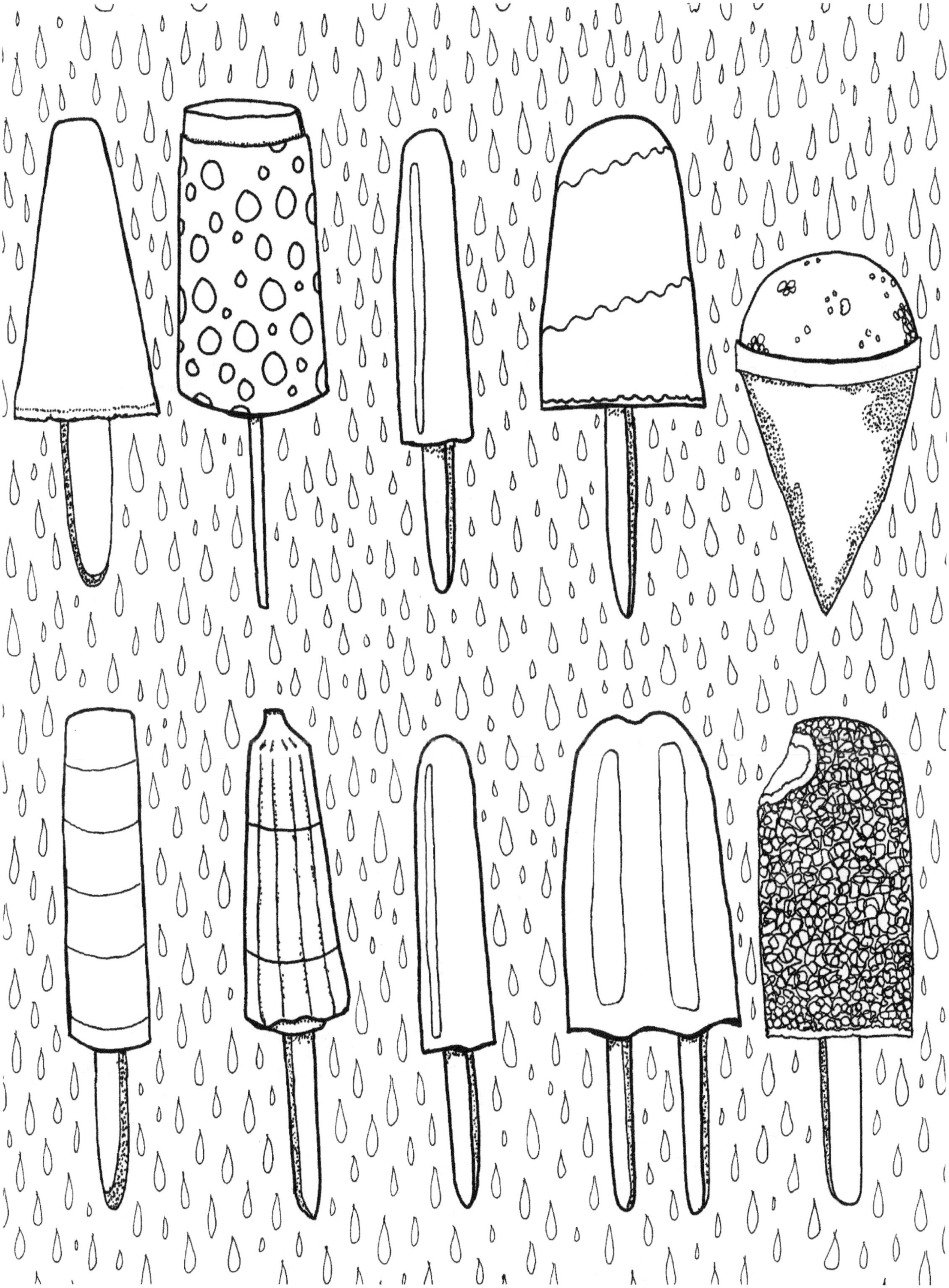

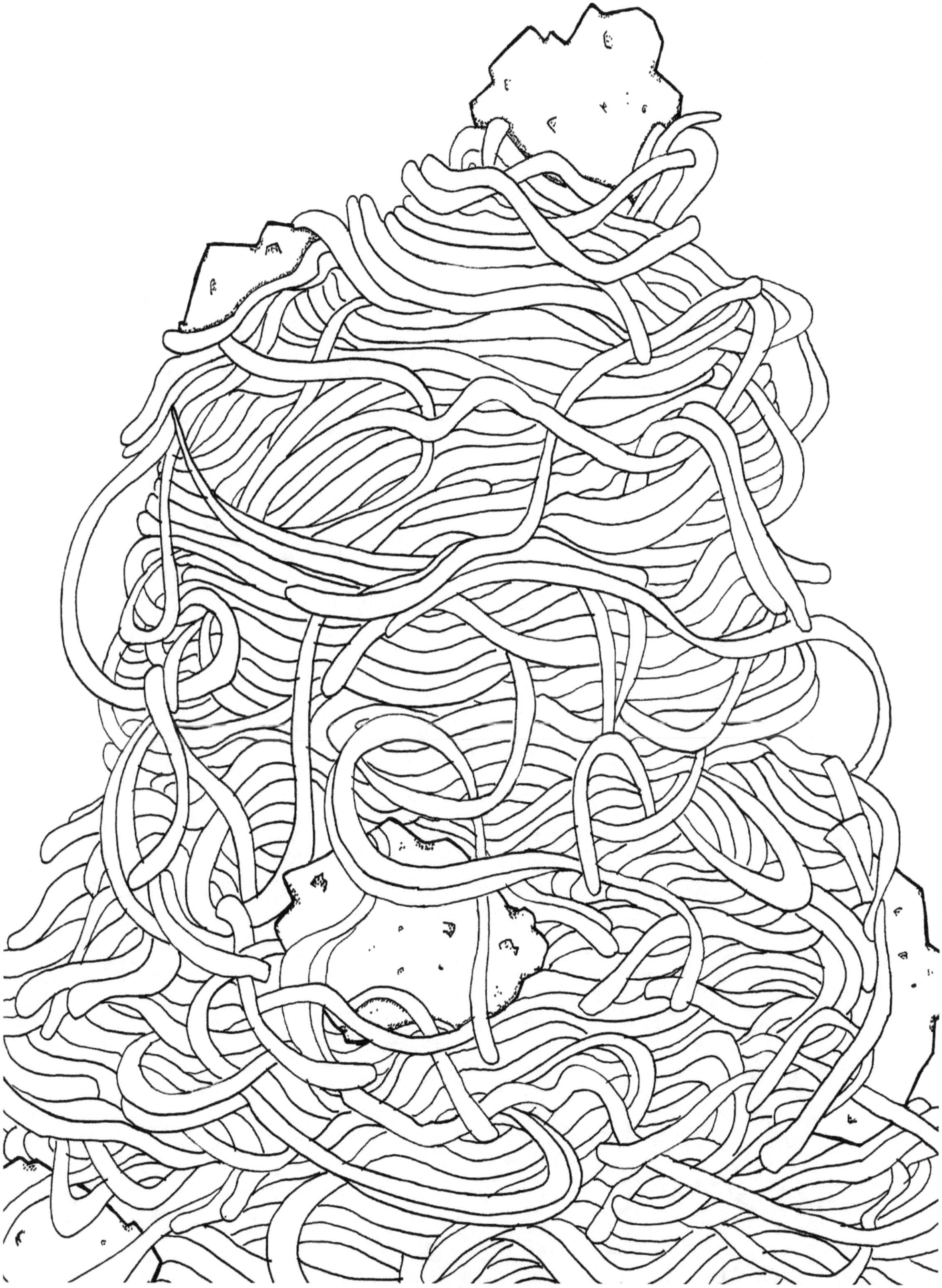

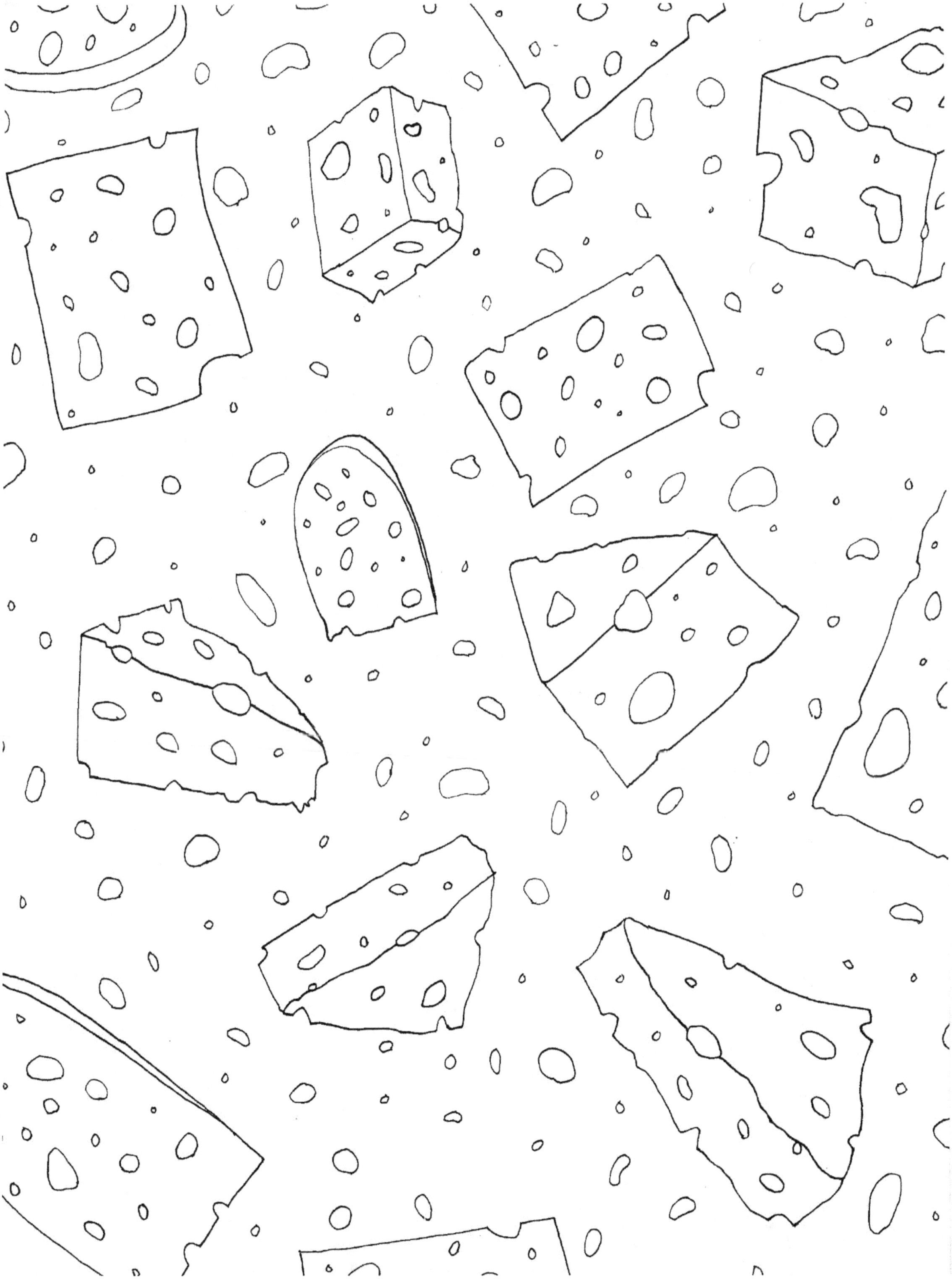

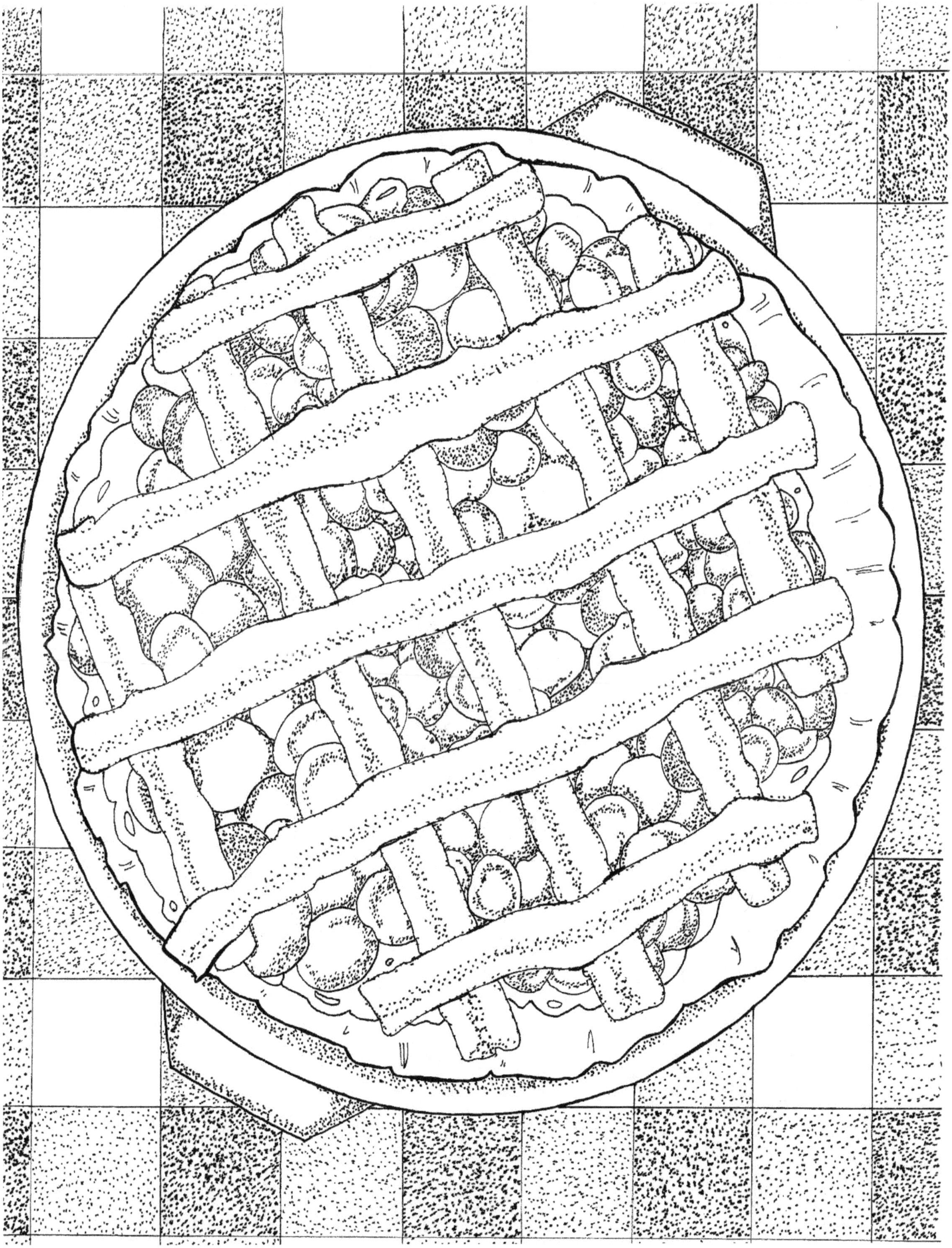

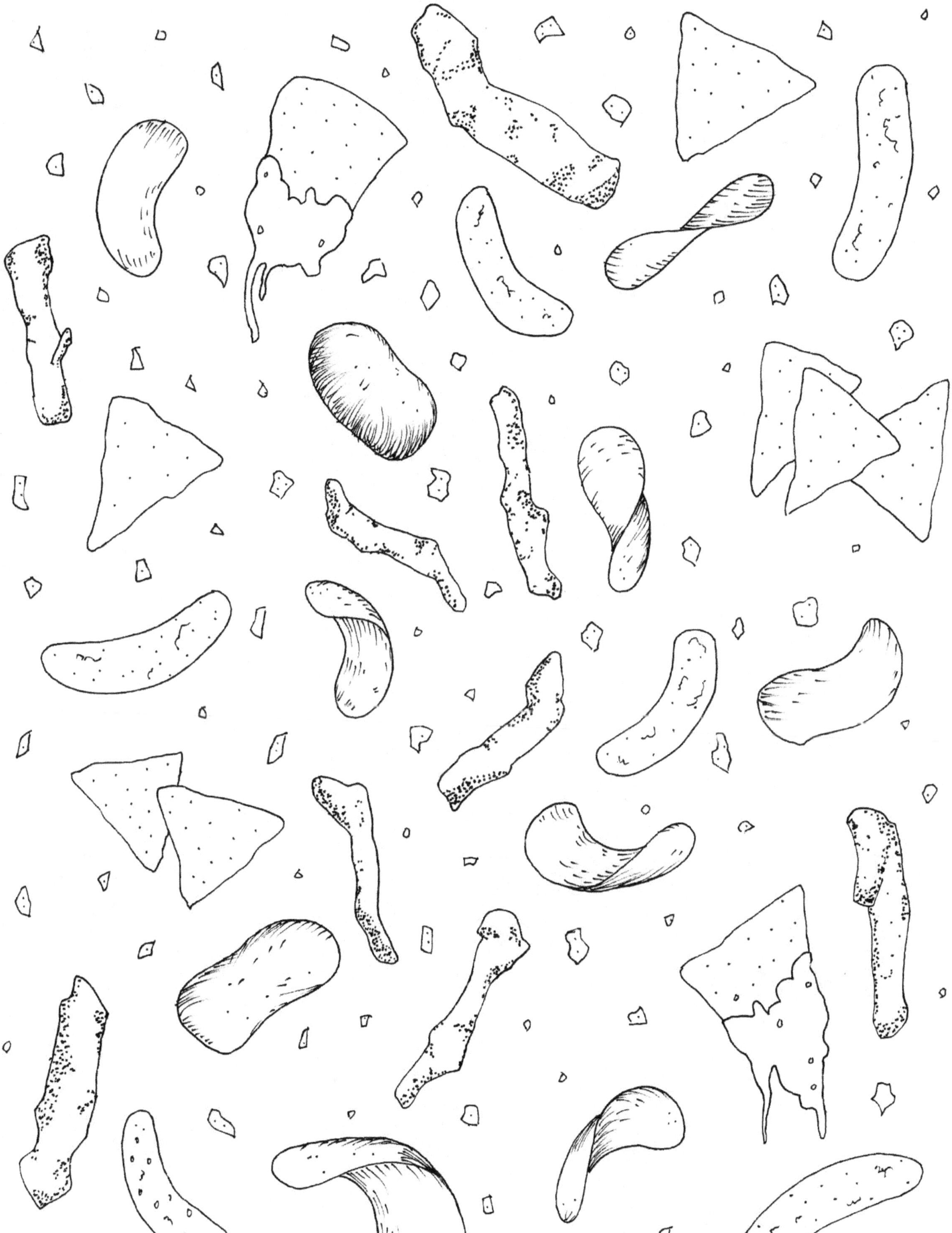

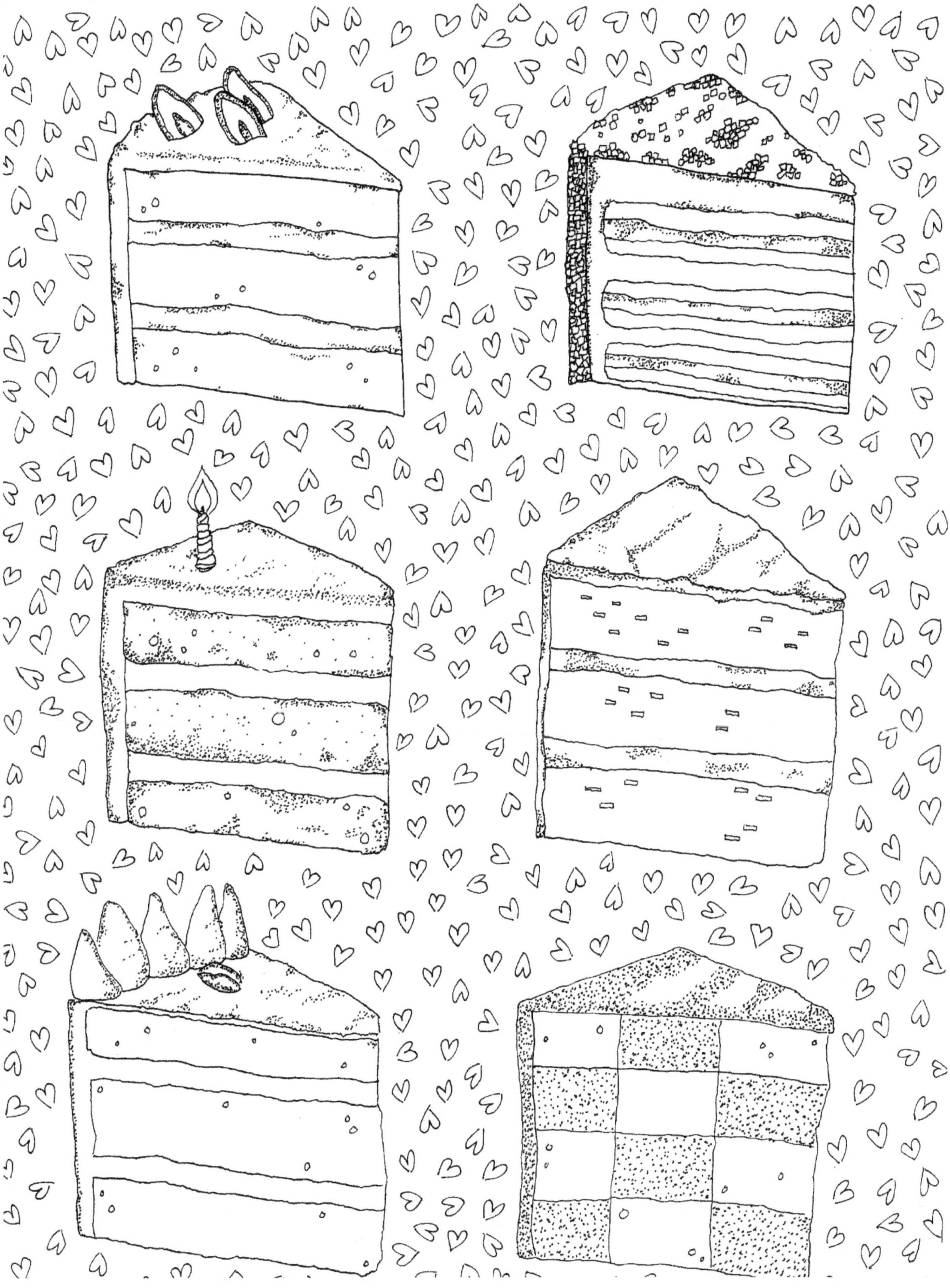

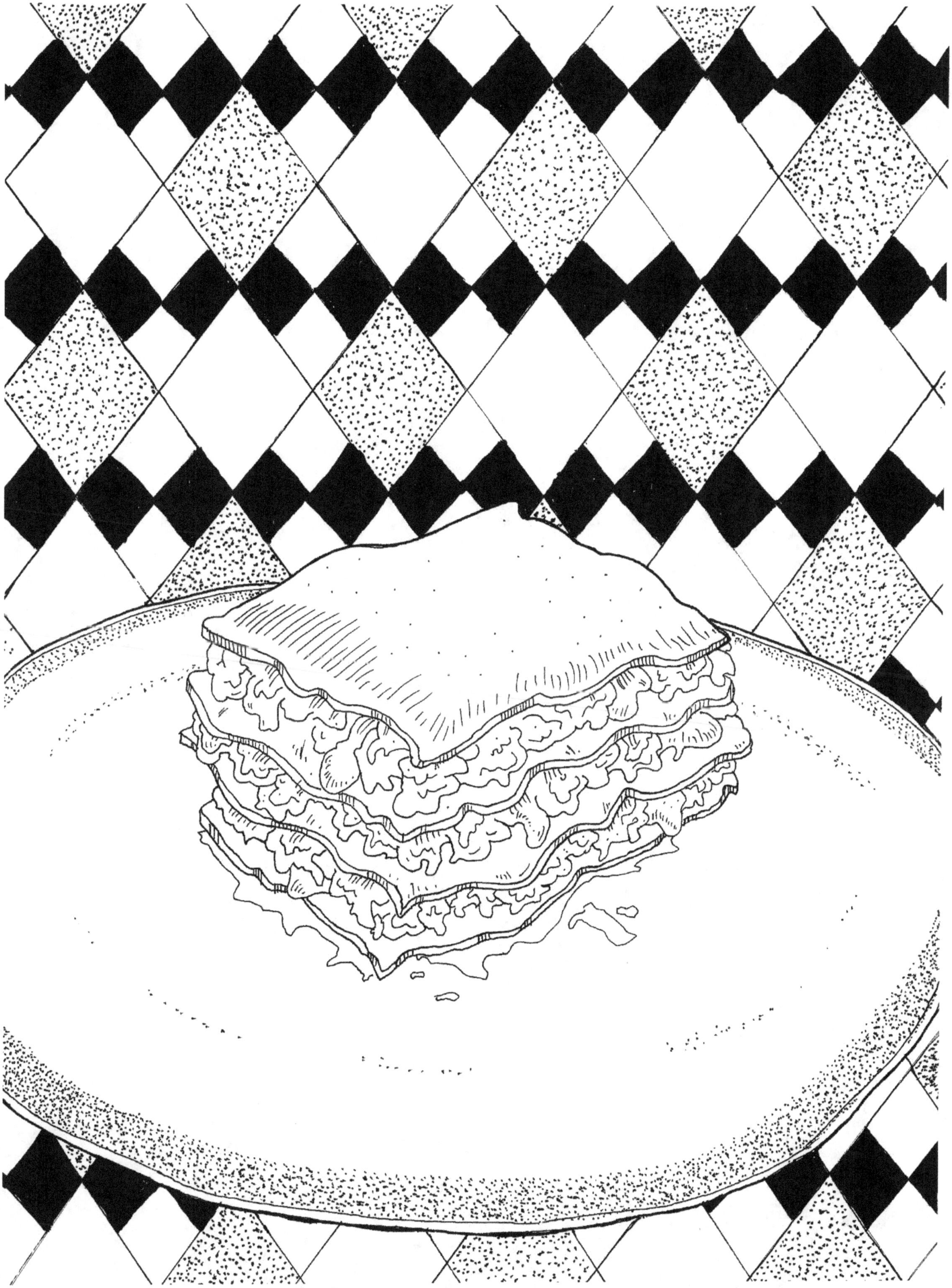

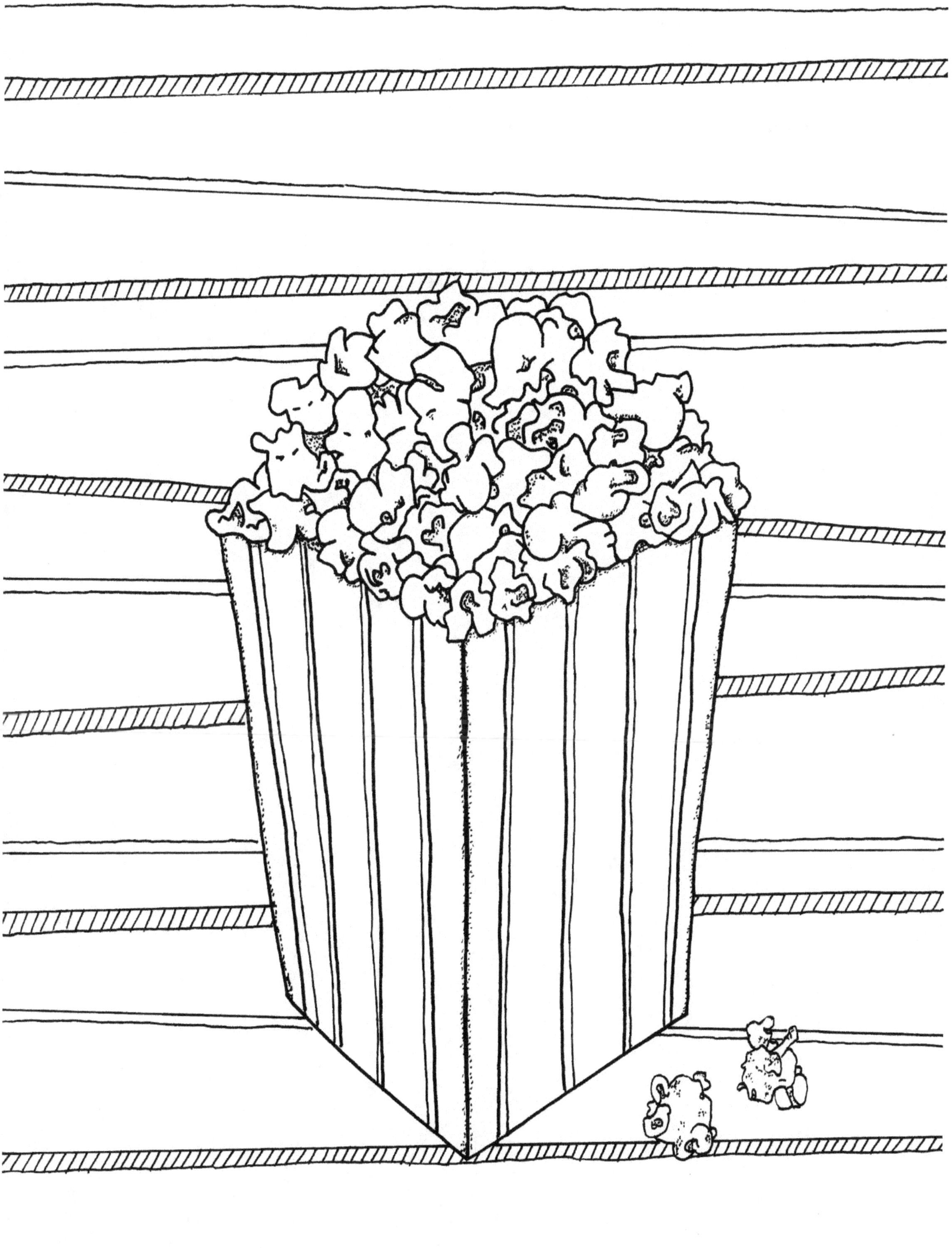

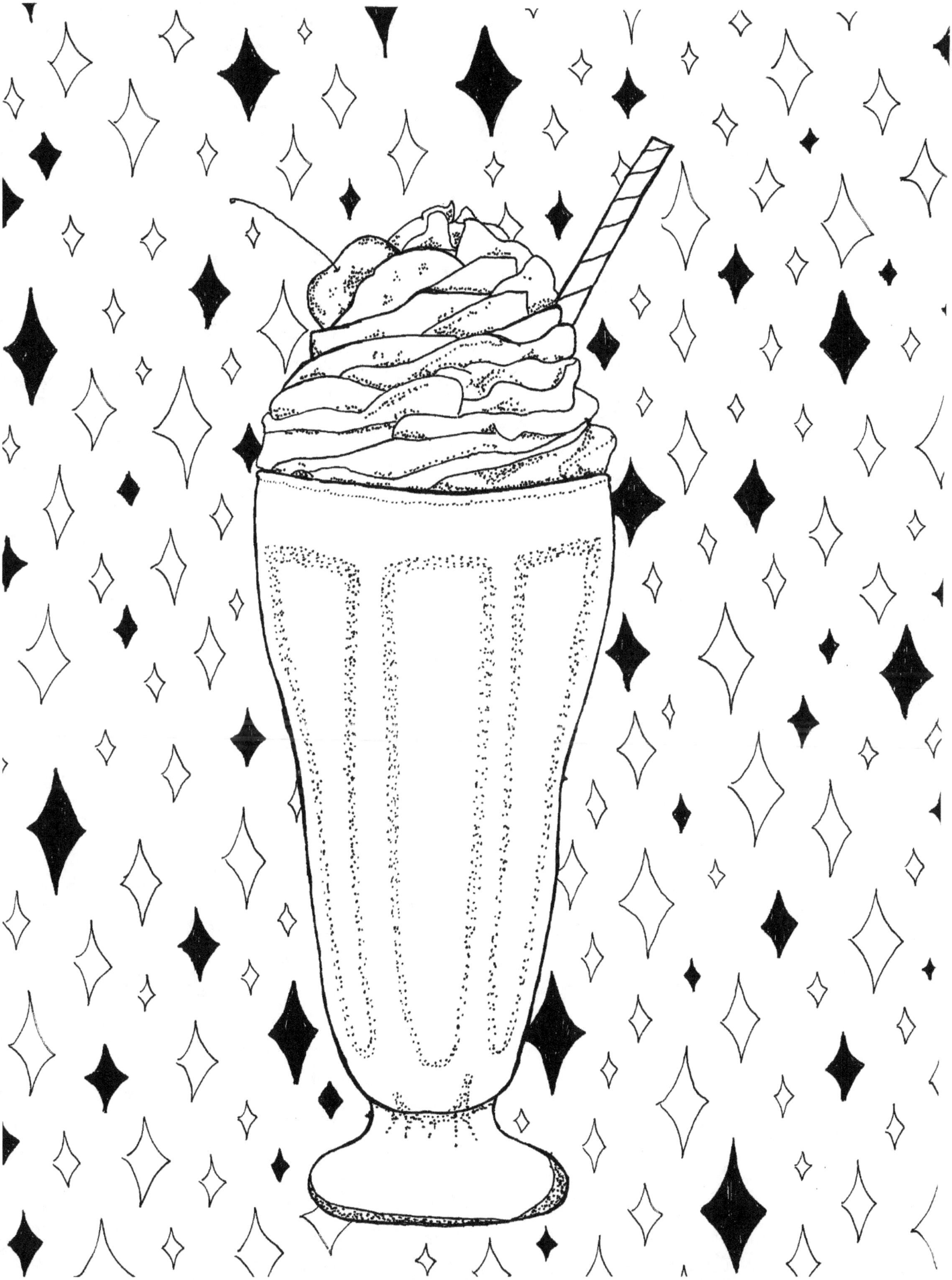

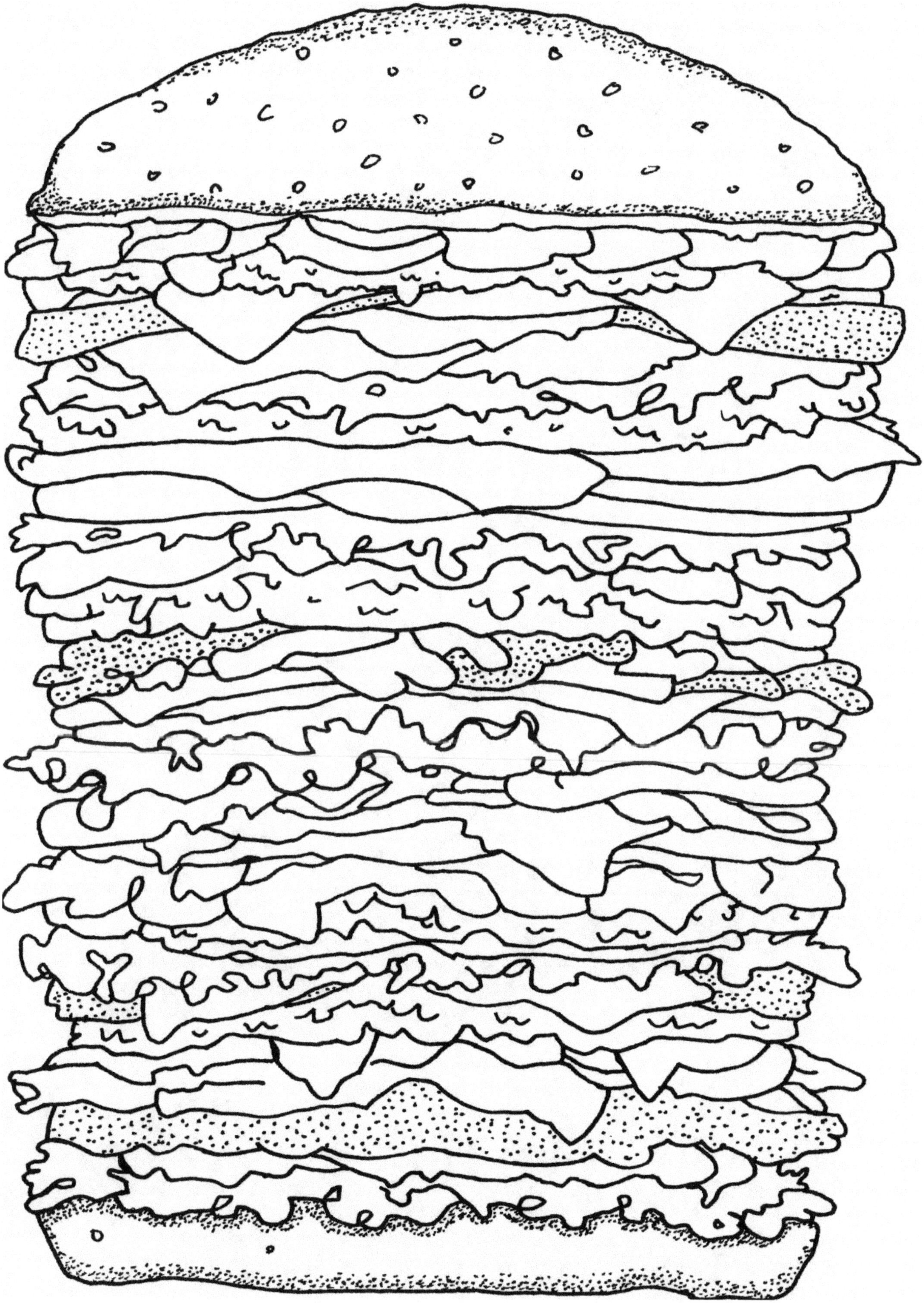

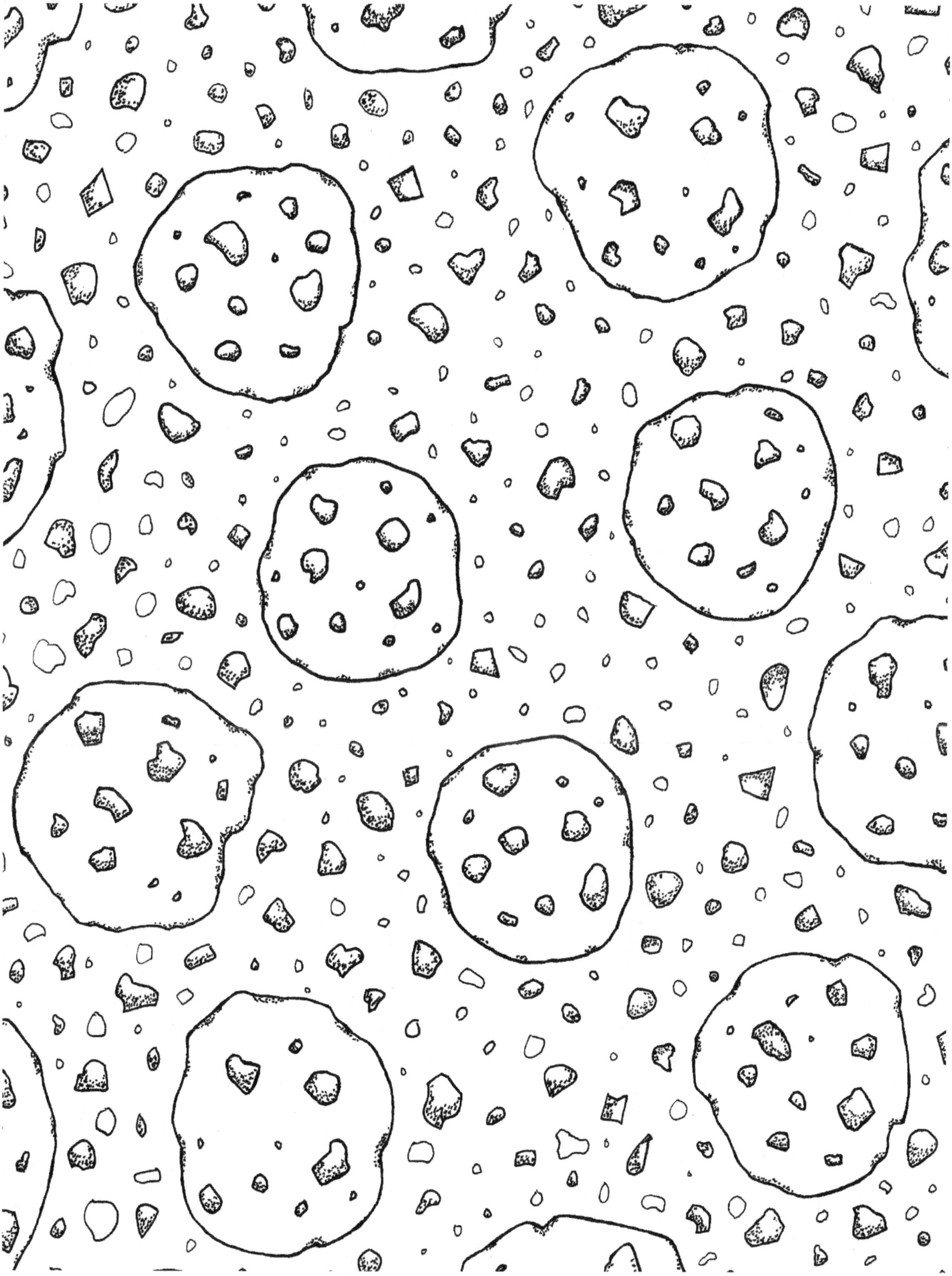

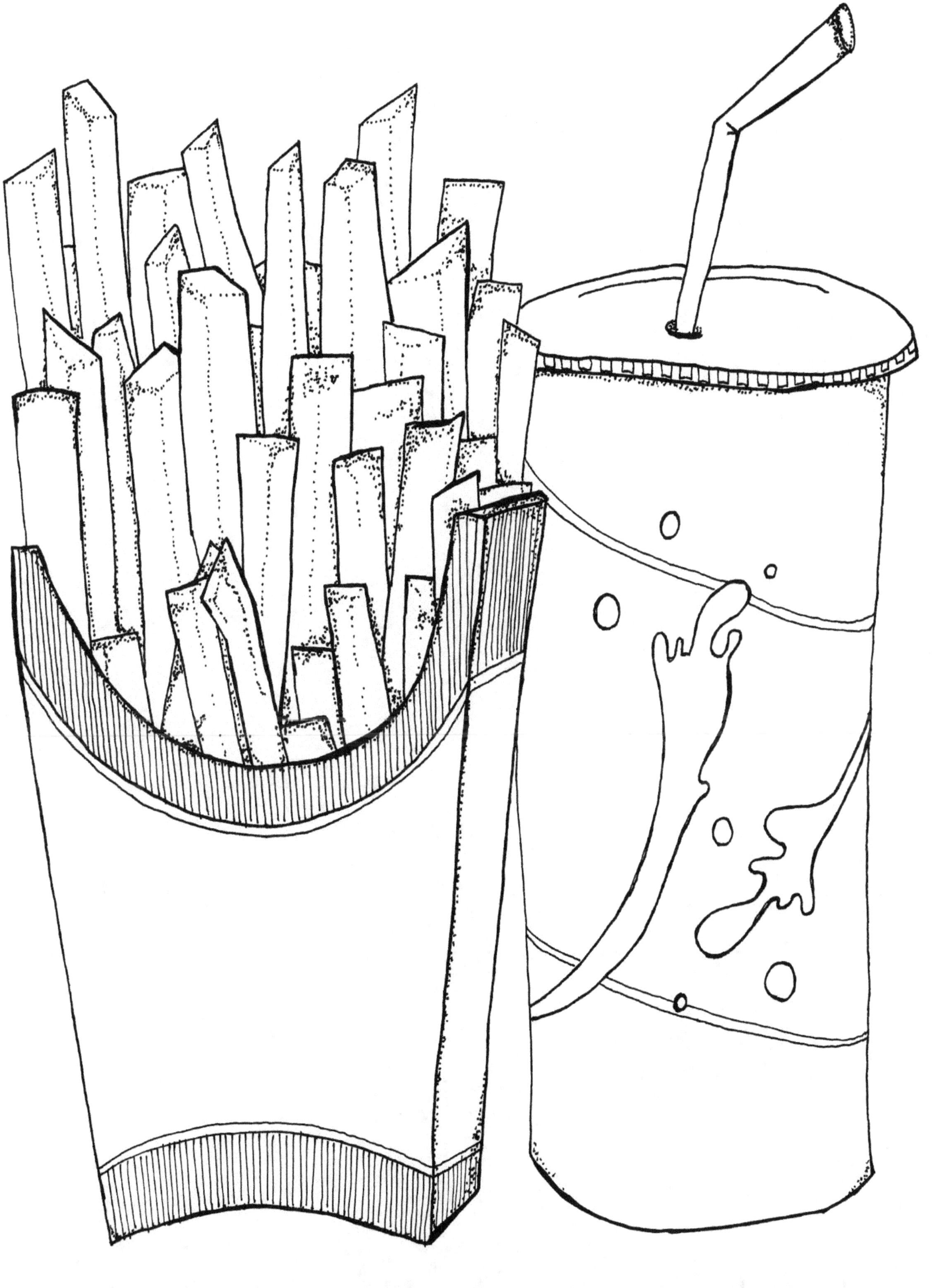

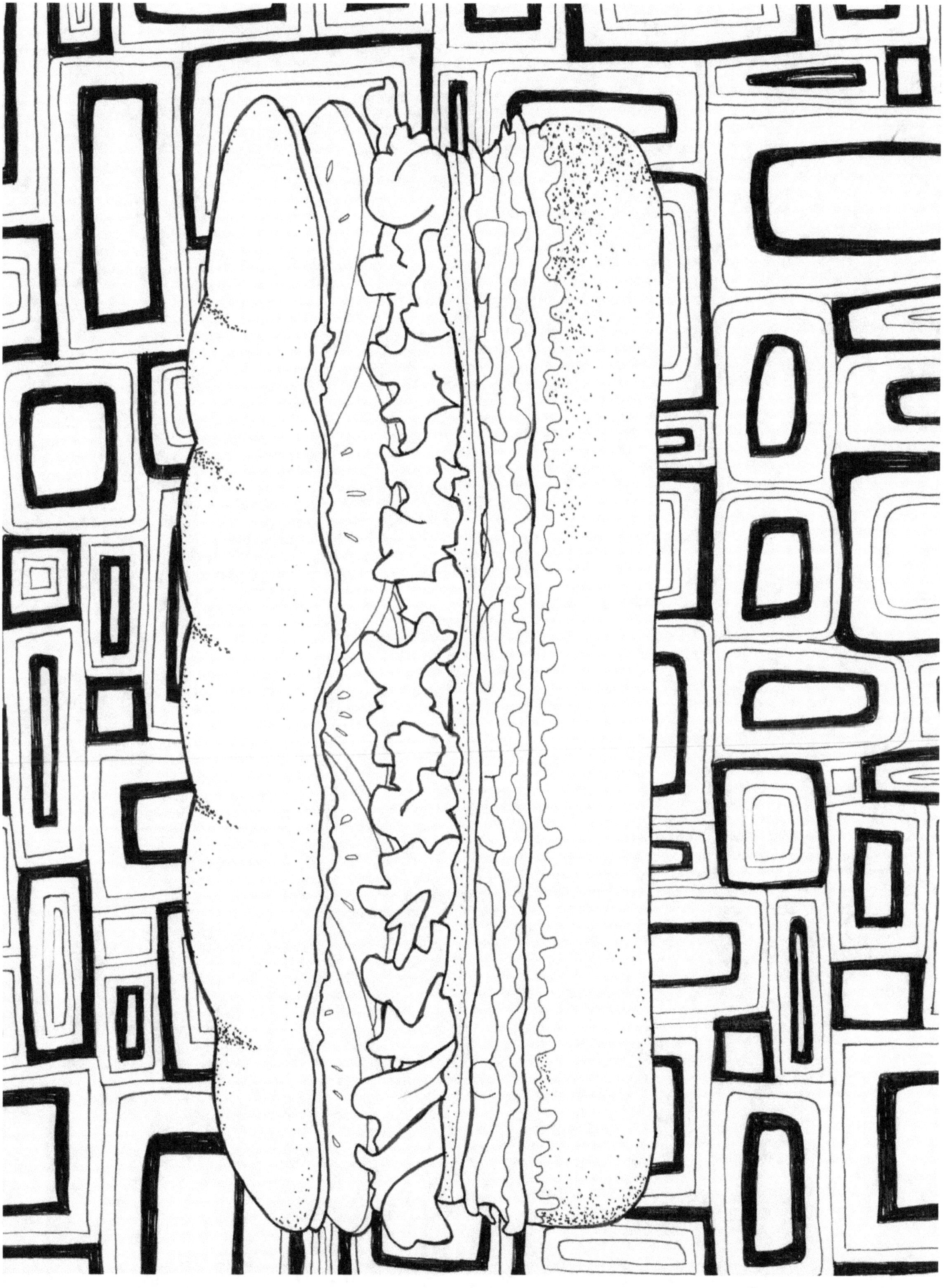

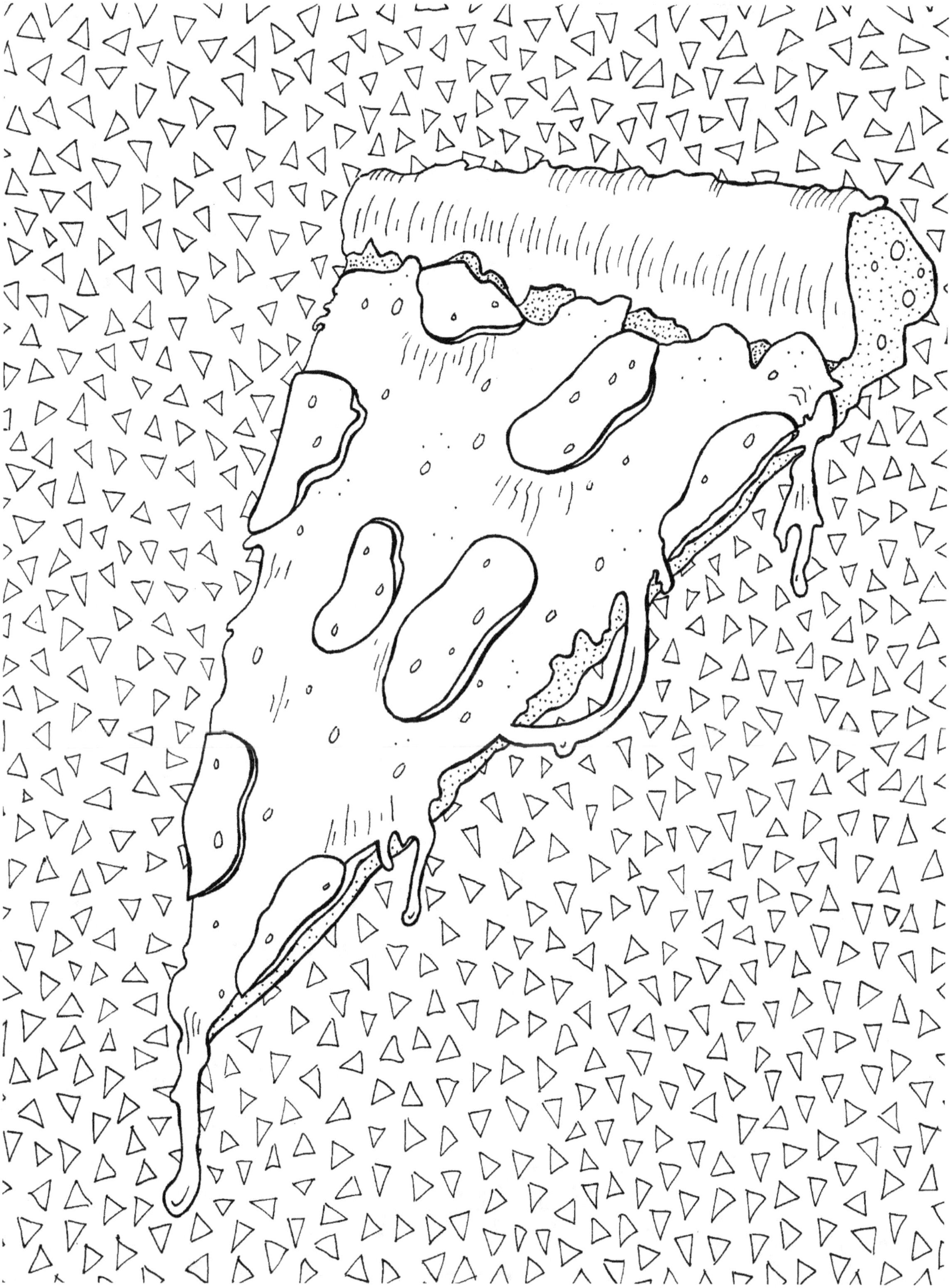

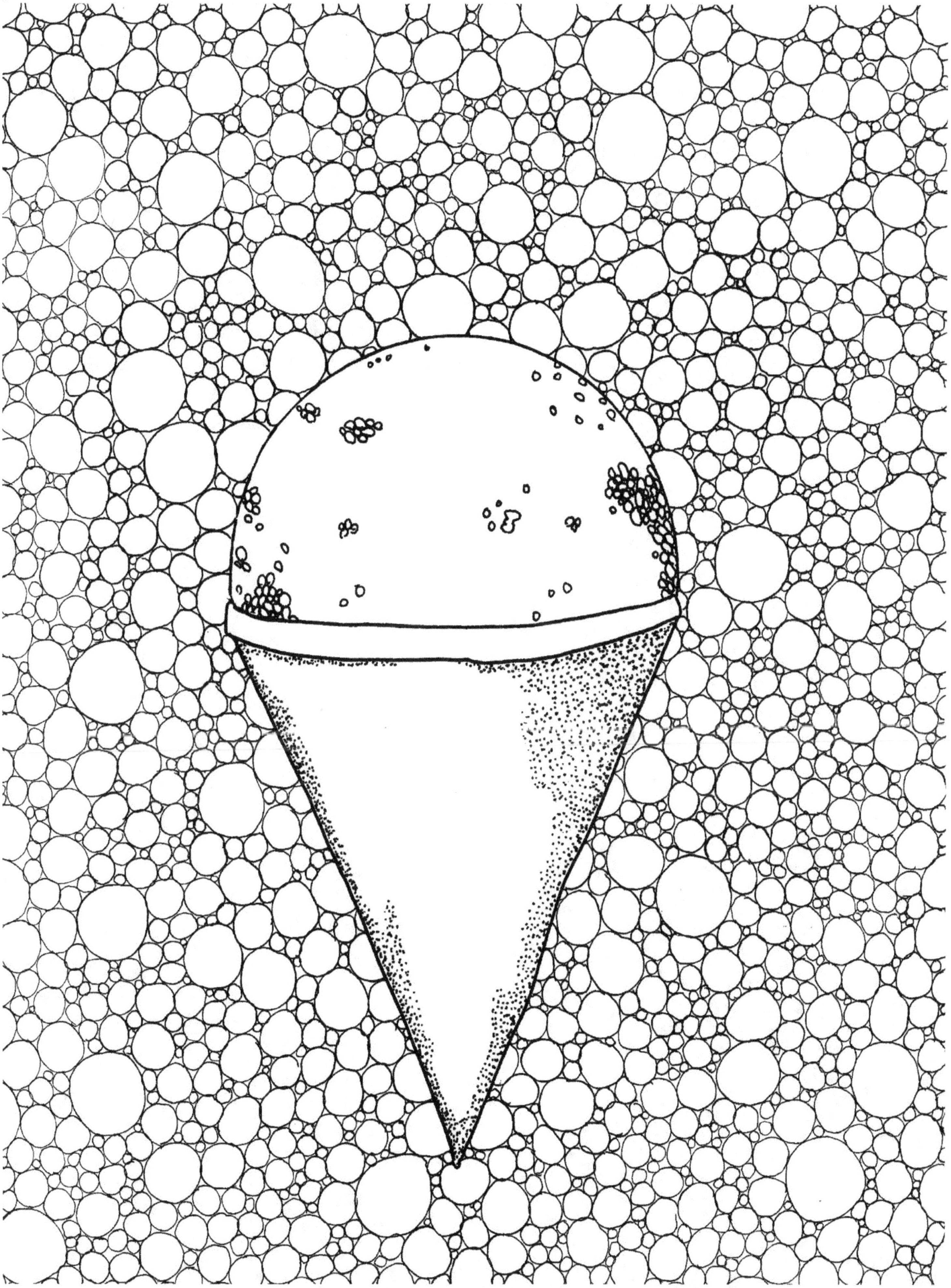

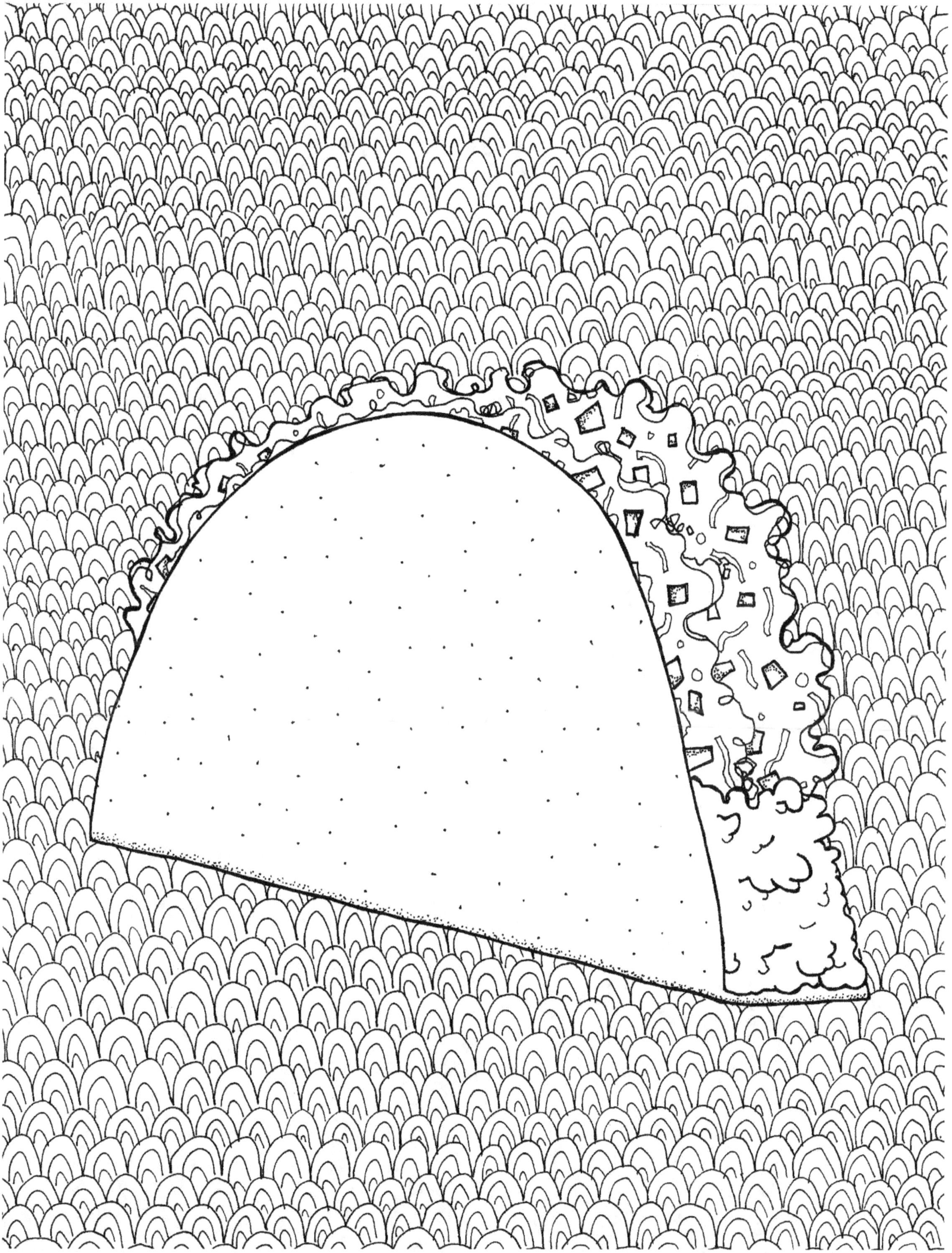

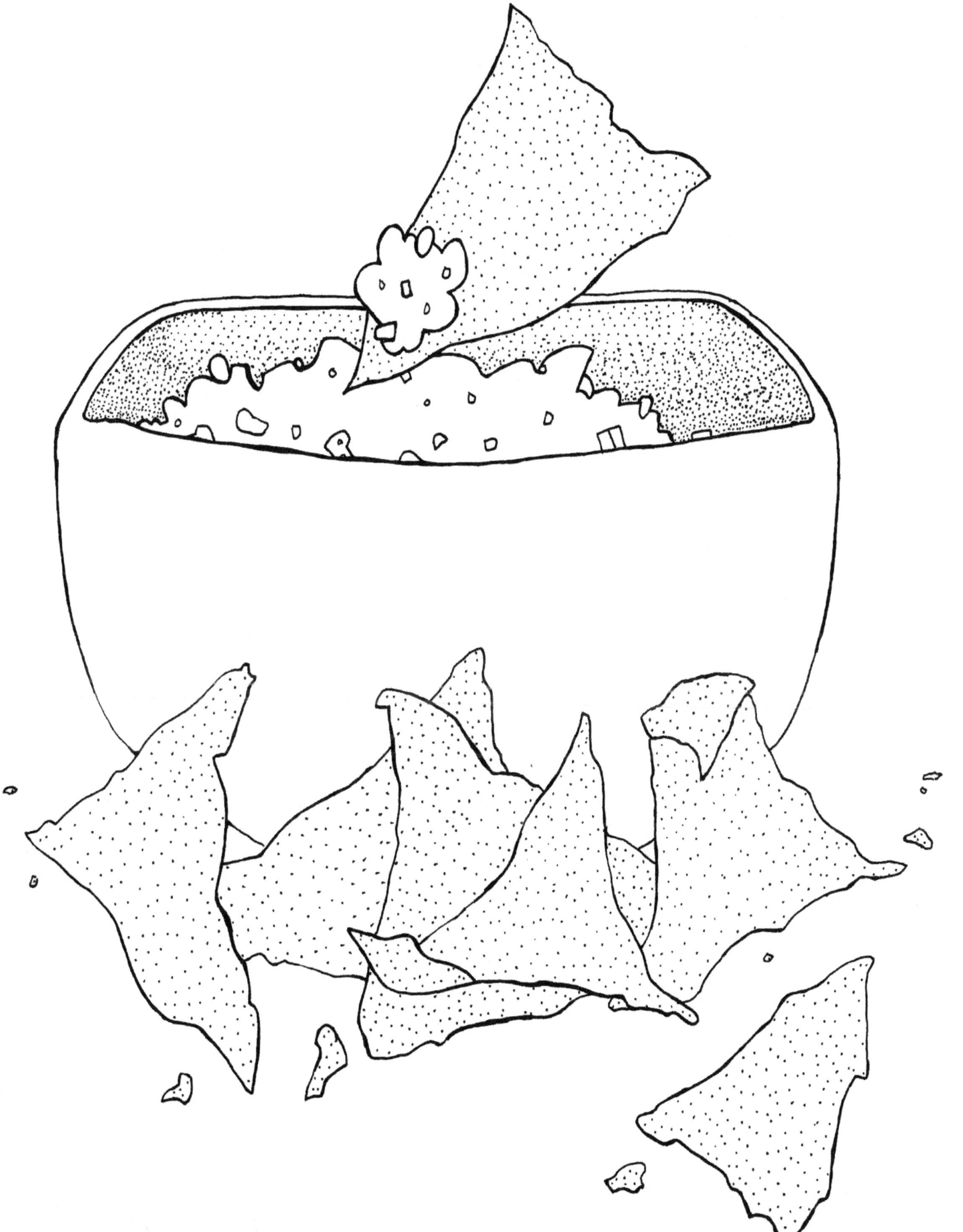

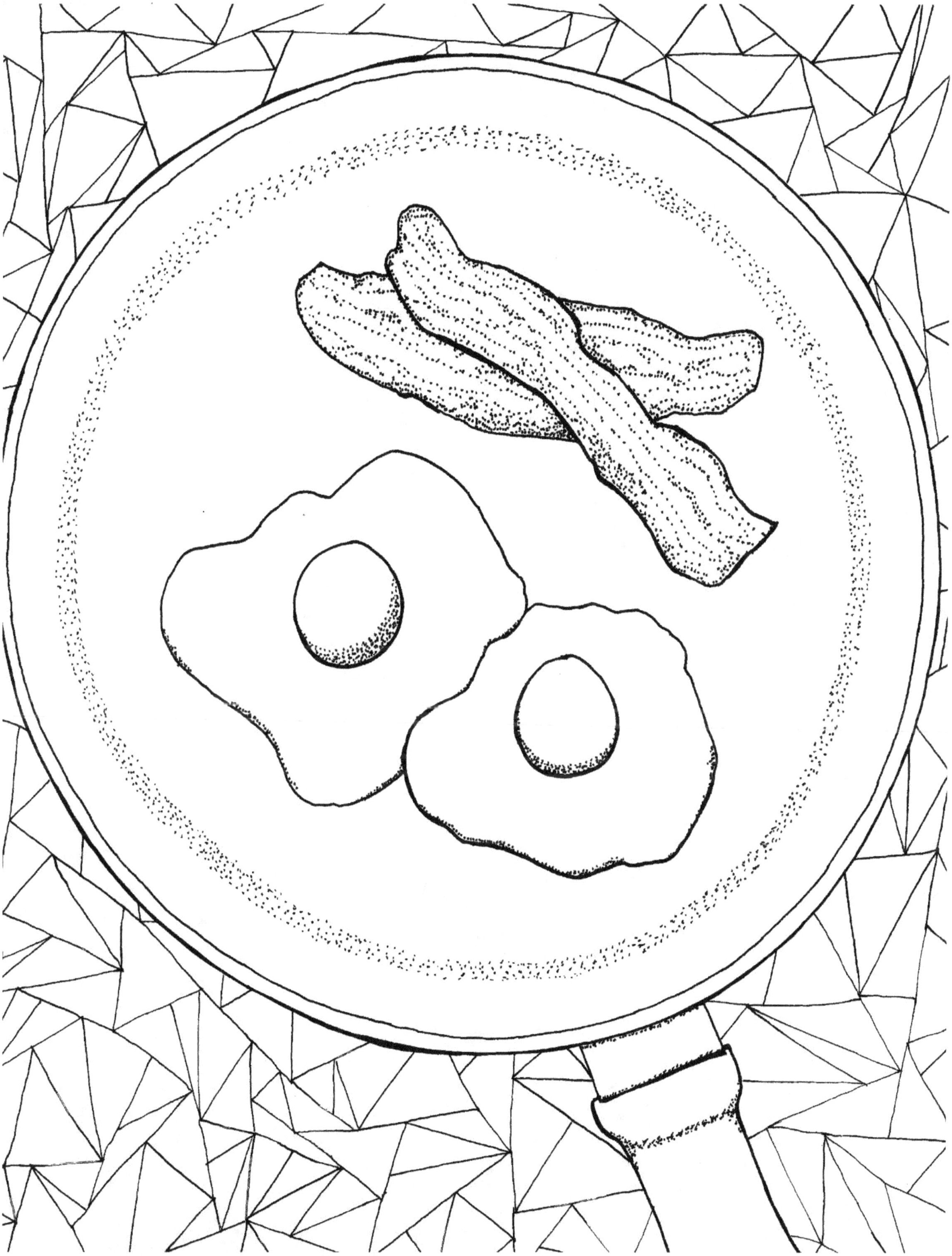

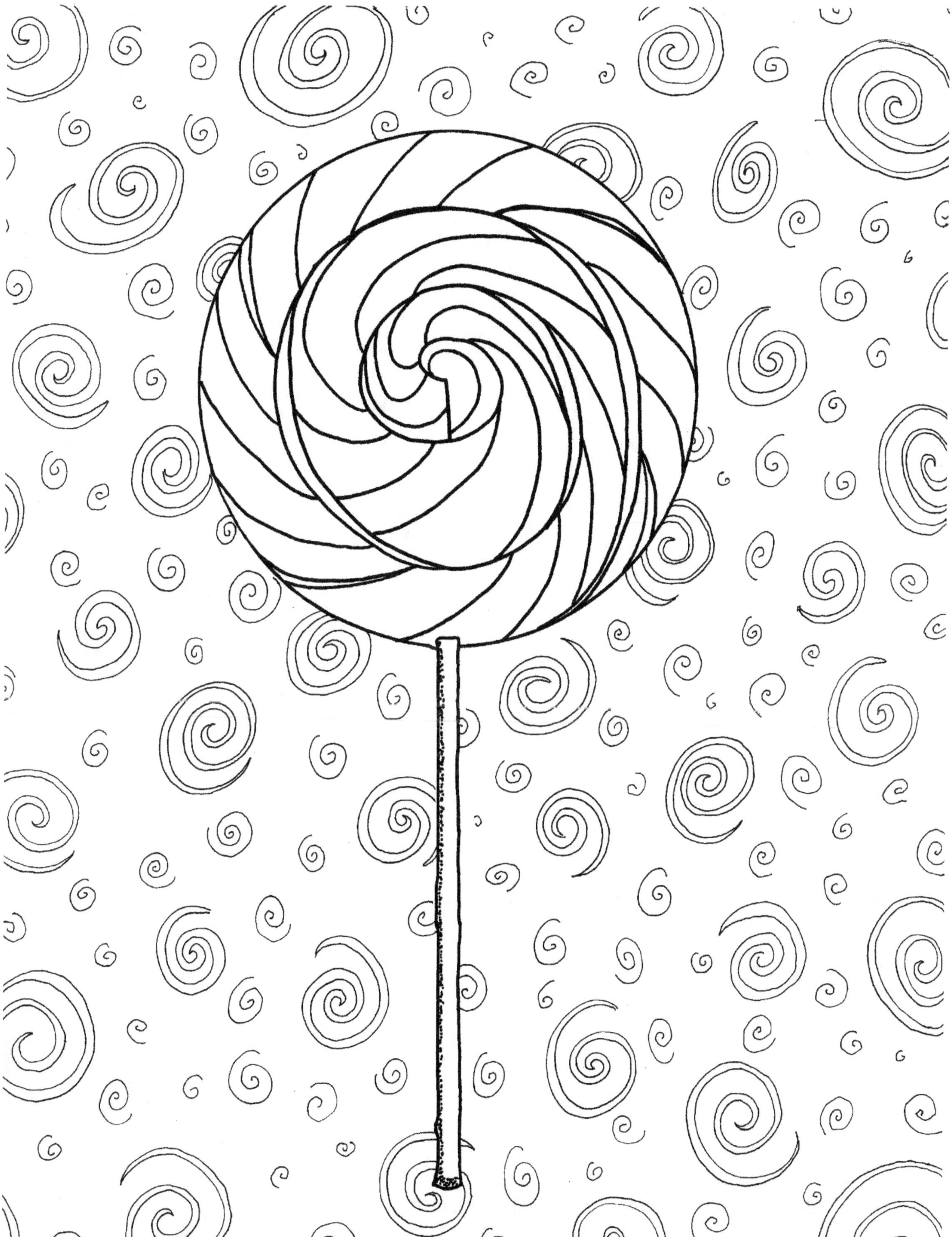

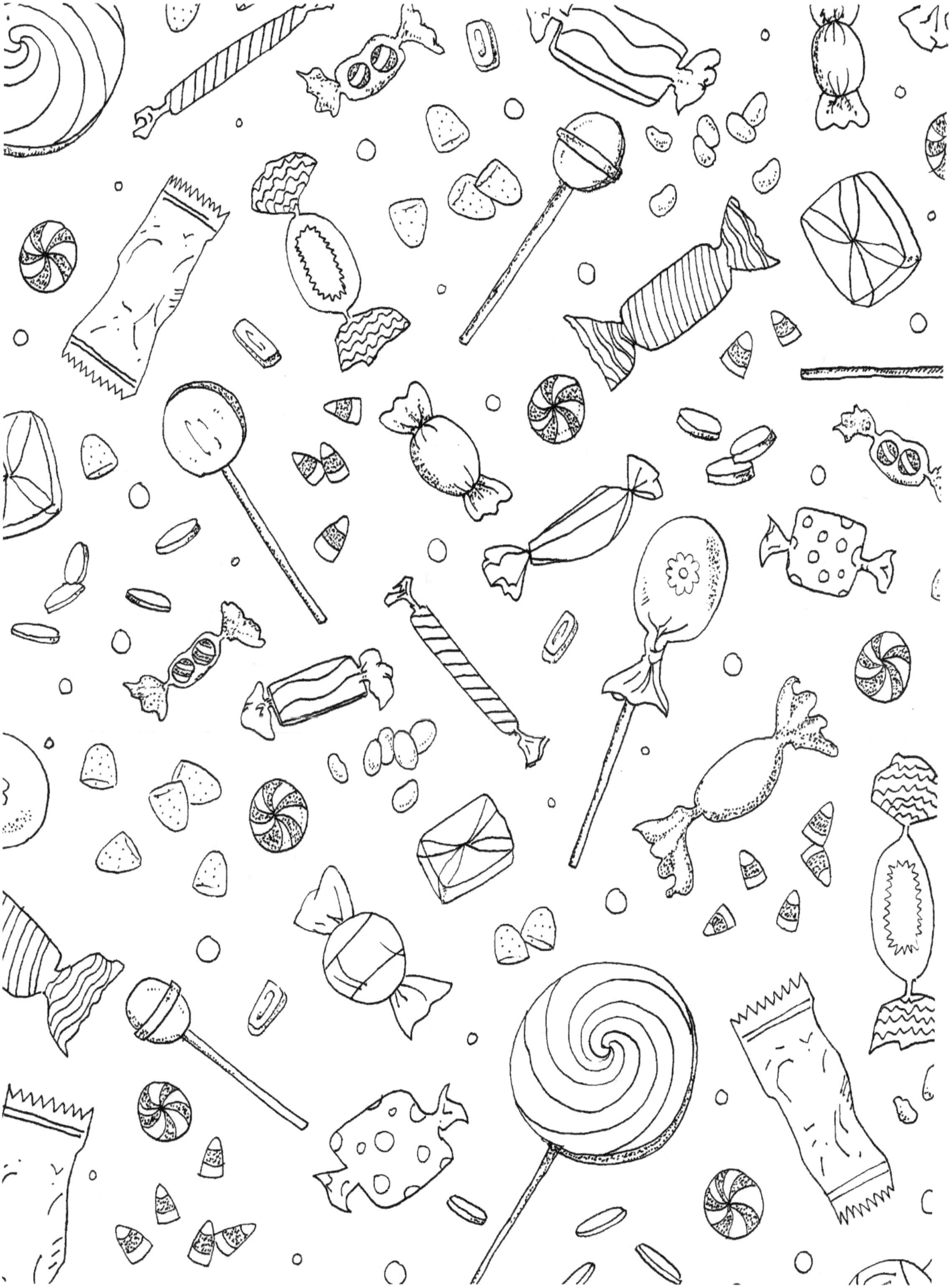

www.ingramcontent.com/pod-product-compliance
Lightning Source LLC
Chambersburg PA
CBHW081018170526
45158CB00010B/3085
* 9 7 8 0 9 9 7 9 9 3 5 0 9 *